Snout

Chasing Tail

Snout

Chasing Tail

Joseph Fulkerson

published by Laughing Ronin Press 2021
Image used under license from Shutterstock.com

"The fourth horseman blazes his own path and solidifies a well-established identity as he continues to grace the earth with the word, and the word is plenty and filled with the ramblings of philosophical musings only an insomniac poet such as Joseph Fulkerson can pull as he's trying to grab hold onto some sense of normal in a world that's been inverted while spinning furiously in circles on A Merry-go-round in Purgatory."

- Tim Heerdink, author of Checking Tickets on Oumaumua, Razed Monuments, The Human Remains, Red Flag and Other Poems, Sailing on the Edge of Time, I Hear a Siren's Call, Ghost Map, and A Cacophony of Birds in the House of Dread

Stonks!

The experts are convinced
it's a bull market
or maybe a bear market
either way
they're certain it's a mammal
with four legs, possibly hooves
but to be safe
they're not ruling out claws.

They are convinced
trickle-down economics *does work*
but only if you have a white collar

-or-

if you've ever attended a
three martini lunch meeting

even more so if you can

write it off as a business expense.

Choosing to buy into this

provides a guarantee of residual income

and a lifetime of resentment

and complacency.

The fix is in;

I'd be remiss if I didn't state the obvious.

A metric shit-ton of regret is in store for you,

mister.

You can't deny

the devil has the best deal

when it comes to plea deals.

He'll get you prime real-estate

on the 9th green of the
9th circle.

You'll be a scapegoat
the fall guy,
caught red-handed
holding a red herring.

You'll be first in line for an ass-whooping
and last in line for your parole hearing.

If the road to hell is paved with
good intentions, then the road to heaven
is littered with anal fissures.

The saying goes "if you mess with the bull
you get the horns."

They failed to mention the bull cock.

You're prime ass, prime meat
in prime time

delicate sensibilities are a delicacy
in the prison yard.

You'll be sewing golden parachutes
into white collars
in your sleep
in no time.

It's a bull market after all.
Or was it bear?

Luck Favors the Risk Takers

although

       I'll venture

a guess

          the corpse

at

the

bottom

of the chasm

       would disagree with that statement

Wrong in all the Right Places

People claim they want honesty,
but they're scared of the truth.

They want advice without an opinion.

They want their courage tested
without the struggle
associated with it.

They want patience
and they want it now!

They want talent,
yet are unwilling to put in the work
necessary to bring it forth.
It hurts wrong in all the right places.

I 🖤 Tyler

Doive?

Duvet?

What's the difference

it's a fucking blanket.

Snout Chasing Tail

Can you understand the desperation
of the inner self?

Can you empathize with the plight
of a man who has no direction or plan?

Will you sympathize with the man
helping to circumvent
the upcoming storm of the soul?

Who can understand this?

It is beyond interpretation
or even comprehension.

My emotions play on an endless loop
snout chasing tail
on a lifelong journey

to the depths of utter contempt
and disdain.

My pen flows as a broken water spout,

pouring onto the page, flooding the world
with my words.

My thoughts many
yet answers are few

meditating thoroughly
but speaking sparingly.

I am forever lost
in the desert of my mind.

To My Former Self, from a Future Iteration

You should write this down.
Actually, you should write
everything down
all the time.

On Oct 12th, 2022
at approximately 5:30pm
when you get to Jimmy John's,
order the *Beach Club* instead
of the *Totally Tuna.* You'll be
glad you did.

Don't stop by the bank to withdraw
cash from the ATM.

It will eat your card, forcing you
to use your MasterCard
the rest of the week.

Instead of meeting Matt
to have a drink, stay home.

If you absolutely insist on going,
don't stay out too late.
10:30-11pm at the latest.

When you get to the pub,
sit at the fifth bar-stool from the door.
The one directly in front of the taps.

At exactly 8:35pm order an old-fashioned
with Jameson and sip until gone,
ignoring the girl with the nose ring
who's new to town.
You'll thank me later.

Just enjoy the karaoke
and have another drink
or two, if you like.

Now whatever you do, do not
make eye contact with the woman
directly behind you at your 5 o'clock.

Don't watch as she takes a drink
and laughs with that blonde friend
of hers, all the while making sure
you're paying attention
 out of her peripherals.

DO NOT engage in small talk.
As a matter of fact, don't talk
to anyone at all.

If you do, you will find her

witty and funny and sexy as hell.
Resist.

You will know her voice
like the melody to a song
you can't quite remember,
but that you never want to forget.

Please, please don't give her your number.

Resist looking into her hazel-colored eyes,
try not to fall in love
with the way she bites her bottom lip
while thinking of an excuse
to come back up to the bar.

She'll find one, and make her way
back to where you sit.

She will be everything we've been looking for;
everything we need.

We will fall in love with her instantly.

We will propose quickly,
get married quicker
and live a happy life
for a long time, that is
until the cancer takes her from us.

It will be the hardest thing
we will ever encounter.

You will consider death to be easier,
and I'm not so sure it wasn't
                          -isn't-
which is the reason for this
highly irregular correspondence.

So do us both a favor,

don't go to karaoke night on

Thursday October 12th, 2022.

It's too much of a loss.

Stay home and watch **_Broad City_** instead.

(this week's episode is quite funny)

You will thank me later.

Sincerely,

Future Iteration of Us

Debutant

You're a miracle of debauchery

a debutant

a fuck boi

they're lining up

begging you

to grab them by the pussy

you're a rapscallion

a trailblazer

a ram scaling the crags

up the side of the mountain

a trendsetter

a taste maker, king maker

a bellwether and

a broke-dick bloat
of a bloke.

Good riddance,
Agent Orange

The Space Between

There is a difference
between education and experience
motivation and dedication
understanding and enlightenment.

Although often confused
one for the other
the space between is vast,
immeasurable even.

Both Buddhist and Christian
Muslim and Hindu
Jew and Hari Krishna

all believe in a higher power—
a mother

a father, a deity

their paths to enlightenment
to salvation
Nirvana,
are as varied and conflicted
as the cluster of stars in the heavens.

The United States of Dichotomy

We are urban playgrounds
And rural homesteads

We are inner city concrete jungles
And rolling Appalachian hills

We are Wall Street,
Main Street

A backcountry road
With the windows down

Come one, come all
But
We are building this wall

We are the abused
We perpetrate abuse

We are predators
And the prey

We are instigators,
Propagators

A tourniquet
On the arm of justice

We are innocent
We are the accused

We are propaganda
We are fake news

We've made an institution
Out of infatuation with half-truths

We are the privileged
As well as the underrepresented

We are white privilege

We are the gentrification of all

We are law enforcement

We are racial profiling
We are *stop and frisk*
We are discrimination

We are a *no-knock warrant*
To the wrong apartment

We are the protester
And the establishment
Which is protested against

We are unrest and upheaval in the streets

We are the distilled will of the masses

We are legion

We are the upper class
The lower class
And everything in-between

We are the middle child
The only child

The chosen
And
Lost generation

We are first generation,
Second and third
Generation citizenship

We are the perpetrator
And the arbitrator
Of justice and injustice

We are jihad realized
Sadism exemplified
Unmitigated terror
The wager of wars

We are the land of opportunity

And mistakes

We are rising to the challenge

We are the envy of many a nation

The balm of Gilead
We are democracy

We are more than the sum of our parts

We lead by example

We are hope and optimism

We are free and fair

We are stand up

And be counted

For what we believe in

We are neighbor

Helping neighbor

We are

Bipartisanship

Biracial

Bisexual

Bilingual

Nondenominational

Multicultural

And

By the way

We are on the verge of something great
If we could just get out of our own way.

Wad of Flesh

What are we

but a spark of consciousness

        encased in a wad of flesh

walking around bumping

into one another?

Lost in Translation

in transit,
wide-eyed stares
blank expressionless faces

shifting eyes foretelling the incapacity
to relate to the poured out souls
of the next generation

buildings abandoned, condemned
housing projects, playgrounds
rusted into non-existence

we all share the blame
for this generation's
refusal to grow up;

more accurately their inability
to break through the confines
of adolescence and become
the torch-bearers
we all need them to be.

Fan Mail

After reading your posts for the past several months, I've realized you are one of the many reasons this country is going to shit. Now I do realize we didn't have much of a choice on the ████████ this year or the past several elections, but ████ doesn't even know where he is half the time, nor remembers what he's even running for...this is really the best person the ████████ party could come up with to run a country? I would be completely embarrassed if I was a ████████ and that's all I had to offer the country. Found out there are 72.1 million stupid people in America and when seeing this I realized it truly doesn't matter....this country is already fucked by all you libtards anyways. So cheers to you 👊 for helping fuck this country even more.

It doesn't matter who the ████████ is, its the direction in which this country is going. ████████ can't do much without the ████ backing, so that's not my worry. Just remember my words in 10 years. I pray to God I'm wrong.

Didn't even take 10 years 😂

What are you talking about?

You loving ▇▇▇ and him being the best thing ever....
How's that working out? 😂 🤣

No complaints here.

I haven't heard one person that is a leftist mention anything about ▇▇▇ after all the things he has done. Lol people hated one man and they elected the fall of the United States. What has he done to help us? Are you that blind man? I never would've ever seen this out of you.
You're pulling my leg, right?

I'm still waiting for you to tell me all the great things he has done for you and our families

Cause I can tell you about 35 things he has done against it. You damn libtards base everything off emotion not off facts.
Sounds like you all are changing into women. 👧

Well, I'm glad you were able to get that off your chest, bud. I don't need to go around broadcasting my views to feel better about myself.

I'm still waiting...I'm proving a point
Tell me all these great things...I'm all ears.

Okay you do that if it makes you feel better. I don't have anything to prove to you man.

I just want to know what he's doing that is helping us? Can't admit you are wrong can ya....just like a woman 😂 You take care of yourself Josephine. 😂

Wow, sexist much? Sounds like you're having a really bad day. Not that you care, but you're destroying the good will built up between us.

I just thought you had common sense man, again I would've never pegged you as a liptard until this ███ thing came up. You seemed like a great guy with his head on straight but now I see because of people like you is the reason this country will fall. You will see it happen just like it has already started too. I'm very disappointed in you, not that it matters. But if this affects us so be it, doesn't bother me man. I just need to get me a flip phone, buy me a lot of land in the country and live as a hermit. Think I'd be a lot happier. Take care

Sounds like you've had a bad go of it lately. Hope things turn around for you. You take care too.

The Mechanism

A pearl starts as
an irritant to the oyster.

It's the oyster's triggered response
that creates this object of beauty.

A diamond is created
under extremes of
temperature and pressure

which over time results
in the hardest stone known to man.

Suffering is the mechanism
the catalyst
for inspiration

for in the balance
of suffering's scales
all of life is weighed.

Successes, failures
good and not so good choices
all more poignant when viewed
through its lens.

Genuine, unadulterated suffering
most of us will never know
yet often that is what
separates the mundane
from the divine.

Death Comes on Twelve Wings

The botched second coming
of the tentacle-clad monolith
                    descended
from the brothel in the clouds

like a child's discarded plaything
its innards exposed
for the world to see.

Multitudes dying
cancerous deaths,
tapeworm filled vomit
venom sac lungs
ending our cradle death

with a raspy air
of finality.

An absentee father on bedrest
is exposed to all sorts of chemicals
straight from the needle's dripping stem.

Don't make liars out of us, Daddy.
You always were the one to choose
which life to take next.

Knife wounds never heal as they should
edge jags to edge, unhealed flesh
puckering away from itself
in stubborn refusal.

The switchblade cuts
to the bone quick
blood geysers dance

to the rhythm of the heartbeat

arterial sprays warming
the aching gullet
of my lecherous mouth.

Then there's no stopping my lust.
Therapeutic isolation is
the only way to do it.

No love lost as they say.

I've become the harbinger
of dismay, the calculated risk
that you're willing to stomach

I am the relaxed sphincter
on fresh roadkill

I am the putrid smell

wafting from the closet

where your skeletons reside

I am the tickle in the back

of your throat

and the bad taste

in your mouth

both the allergen

and the antihistamine

I am the word on the tip of the tongue
the thinly veiled threat

I am the mistakes you wish to forget

bastards of an unplanned family

we always wanted

but never could ask for.

All that's left is a kid
face flecked with dirt
staring at the ruddy complexion
of his guardian angel reflected
in the pool of blood.

Blue lights flashing a disco inferno
gives the desired attention
but at what cost?

The gallows cast a long shadow.

The Collective Narrative

In times like these
a man finds himself clinging
to familiar things for comfort.

The economy is in the crapper,
there's a worldwide pandemic
tearing through the streets

and when I sit down to write
I just end up staring at this blank page.

There are things to be said, dammit!

Yet here I sit pondering my dedication
to the word, second guessing

my resolve to do more than exist,
to be more than a cog in the machine

to add a page
a chapter, dare I say
an entire book to the collective
narrative of humanity.

Volcano Tears

A tear falls

from the cheek of a volcano

                              scorching the earth

searing its emotions

into the footprint of history

Priorities today are as follows:

[ ] Milk the cow, but take care to be gentle with the udders (you know how she gets)

[ ] Wash the comforter and sheets-make sure and dry them twice

[ ] Go to grocery-get bananas (the organic kind)

[ ] Pay your mortgage-because you know, foreclosure is a bad thing

[ ] Iron your shirt-dress for the job you want

[ ] Smile and wave

[ ] Be kind, please rewind

[ ] Vacuum the floors-cleanliness is next to godliness

A Merry-go-round in Purgatory

Philosophical   *Theological*   *Economical*

Detrimental   *Emotional*   *Spiritual*   *Eventual*

Irrational

   Occasionally regretful

All words that describe the feelings
I have on a daily basis.

I go from contemplating the mysteries
of the universe, to recounting the most
useless of information, trivial at best.

Such are the cycles of thought
that flow through the mind
on an endless loop

like a merry-go-round

in purgatory.

Screaming into the Night

Sometimes
writing feels like
screaming into
the black of night
with a bullhorn

other times
it feels like
whispering a secret
into the ear
of your sweetheart

-either way-

words are strung together
to form sentences

which form paragraphs
and chapters
in much the same way
they always have

but on the rare occasion

when the stars align
and the muse takes pity

new and exciting ways
are found
to say those things
which cannot be
easily expressed

and that is what
keeps me
coming back
to the page.

The Withered Prince

The face of the withering prince
racked with grief, losses stacking
end over end

multiplying the heartache of
a thousand martyrs
a midlife crisis developing
while we wait

letters crossing continents to find
you lacking, fingers cascading over
the quivering comely parts of another

ecstatic asphyxiation closing tracheal
pathways, bruised with passion
purple and throbbing member

gaining entrance to your fallow earth

elation spewing forth my seed
sown wildly in vain
aching for the gap between us,
between you

swallowing the tonic
I succumb to the bitterness
of complacency.

Never the one to write a eulogy
I feign heartache and tackle the enormity
of my fickle cell anemia,
cells dividing unto senescence.

Seizing the opportunity
I lunge into the abyss

a mere wraith of my former self

alone to the reaches of

Death's scythe.

Sweet Symphony

Creativity is birthed
from the tumult of restlessness
buried deep down in the soul.

It is formed from the shifting
of the tectonic plates within,
from the friction of life
rubbing hard against it.

That rubbing together,
the abrasiveness of the process
churns out the sweet symphony
of the written word.

JWFII

I am a middle child
the only son
two weeks late
for my own birthday

I am riding my bike
through the neighborhood
all day long

I am speed runs of Super Mario Bros
on long summer days

I am passing out Bible tracts
instead of dressing up
or receiving candy on Halloween

I am weeklong tent revivals

in the sweltering Kentucky heat

I am the homeschooled middle school blues

I am too proud to wear hand-me-downs

but too poor to pass them up

I am awkward lovemaking

on the bench seat

of my 85' Chevy S-10

at the drive-in theater

I am naivety and heartache

     I am Toni Braxton's *Never gonna love again*

I am the mended pieces of a broken heart

I am nursed back to health

with the help of my friends

I am R. Kelly's *Ignition the remix*

                    engine raring to go

I am a dumbstruck, love-sick puppy
lost in the unexplored galaxies
that lie within her eyes

I am a newlywed honeymooning
on the wings of angels

I am a proud new father, scared
out of his wits
I am sleepless nights and hazy days

I am weeks
and months
and years removed

              yet

I am restless and unhappy
longing for something else

I am both the cheated on
as well as the cheater

I am divorce and despair
I am all-night sobbing

I am Toni Braxton's *Never gonna love again*

                                    again

I am nursed back to health
with sadness and copious
amounts of alcohol

          I am R. Kelly's *Ignition the remix*
                    back in the saddle
                              once more

I am Joseph 2.0

I am let the pregame begin
the life of the party

I Am the after party

I am 3am breakfast at Denny's
and early morning drunk sex

I am the flavor of the month

I am weeks
and months
and many lovers removed

I am jaded and cynical
and just plain lonely

I am long goodbyes

and starting over

I am cautious optimism
personified

I am hard-earned wisdom
exemplified

I am more than the sum of my parts
I am an amalgam of successes
and failures
but mostly failures

    and

Still here.
Still restless.
Longing for something else.

Honeybee Honey-Do

If I could be

the one

you love

I'd be

a honeybee.

I'd make

a beeline

over

to you,

seeking out

the sweet nectar

within your petals

diving in headfirst

swallowing all I can

filling up

my little

bee pockets

as I went.

Then

I would

hurry back

to the hive

and busy myself

transforming

our love

into a

lifetime supply

of honey.

Joseph Fulkerson runs **Laughing Ronin Press** and is the author of six books. His most recent chapbook, **A Six-pack for Chinaski** was published by **Laughing Ronin Press**. He lives and works in the bourbon-soaked hills of Western Kentucky.

Laughing Ronin Press, LLC
P.O.Box 234
Owensboro, Ky 42303
www.LaughingRoninPress.com

www.ingramcontent.com/pod-product-compliance
Lightning Source LLC
Chambersburg PA
CBHW021143020426
42331CB00005B/879